T0191161

DISCOVERING
CHRISTMAS

A 25-DAY ADVENT DEVOTIONAL WITH ACTIVITIES FOR KIDS

AMANDA JASS

ILLUSTRATED BY MARINA HALAK

Tommy NELSON®

An Imprint of Thomas Nelson

Discovering Christmas: A 25-Day Advent Devotional with Activities for Kids

© 2024 Amanda Jass

Tommy Nelson, PO Box 141000, Nashville, TN 37214

All rights reserved. No portion of this book may be reproduced, stored in a retrieval system, or transmitted in any form or by any means—electronic, mechanical, photocopy, recording, scanning, or other—except for brief quotations in critical reviews or articles, without the prior written permission of the publisher.

Published in Nashville, Tennessee, by Tommy Nelson. Tommy Nelson is an imprint of Thomas Nelson. Thomas Nelson is a registered trademark of HarperCollins Christian Publishing, Inc.

Published in association with the literary agency of WTA Media, LLC, Franklin, Tennessee.

Tommy Nelson titles may be purchased in bulk for educational, business, fundraising, or sales promotional use. For information, please email SpecialMarkets@ThomasNelson.com.

Scripture quotations marked niv are taken from the Holy Bible, New International Version®, niv®. Copyright © 1973, 1978, 1984, 2011 by Biblica, Inc.® Used by permission of Zondervan. All rights reserved worldwide. www.Zondervan.com. The "niv" and "New International Version" are trademarks registered in the United States Patent and Trademark Office by Biblica, Inc.® Scripture quotations marked NIrV are taken from the Holy Bible, New International Reader's Version®, NIrV®. Copyright © 1995, 1996, 1998, 2014 by Biblica, Inc.® Used by permission of Zondervan. All rights reserved worldwide. www.Zondervan.com. The "NIrV" and "New International Reader's Version" are trademarks registered in the United States Patent and Trademark Office by Biblica, Inc.® Scripture quotations marked nlt are taken from the Holy Bible, New Living Translation. Copyright © 1996, 2004, 2015 by Tyndale House Foundation. Used by permission of Tyndale House Ministries, Carol Stream, Illinois 60188. All rights reserved. Scripture quotations marked nasb are taken from the Holy Bible, the New American Standard Bible® (nasb). Copyright © 1960, 1962, 1963, 1968, 1971, 1972, 1973, 1975, 1977, 1995 by The Lockman Foundation. Used by permission. www.Lockman.org. Scripture quotations marked icb are taken from the International Children's Bible®. Copyright © 1986, 1988, 1999, 2015 by Thomas Nelson. Used by permission. All rights reserved.

ISBN 978-1-4002-4896-4 (ebook)
ISBN 978-1-4002-4901-5 (HC)

Library of Congress Cataloging-in-Publication Data

Names: Jass, Amanda, 1986- author. | Halak, Marina, illustrator.
Title: Discovering Christmas : a 25-day Advent devotional with activities for kids / Amanda Jass ; illustrated by Marina Halak.
Description: Nashville, Tennessee, USA : Thomas Nelson, [2024] | Audience: Ages 4-8 | Summary: "Perfect for families celebrating Advent season by focusing on the coming of Christ! Discovering Christmas: A 25-Day Advent Devotional with Activities for Kids uses four key themes of hope, joy, peace, and love to tell the first Christmas story and invite families to focus on the most special reason we celebrate Christmas-the birth of our Savior"-- Provided by publisher.
Identifiers: LCCN 2024005308 (print) | LCCN 2024005309 (ebook) | ISBN 9781400249015 (hardcover) | ISBN 9781400248964 (epub)
Subjects: LCSH: Advent--Juvenile literature. | Christmas--Juvenile literature. | Creative activities and seat work.
Classification: LCC BV40 .J37 2024 (print) | LCC BV40 (ebook) | DDC 242/.33--dc23/eng/20240321
LC record available at https://lccn.loc.gov/2024005308
LC ebook record available at https://lccn.loc.gov/2024005309

Written by Amanda Jass
Illustrated by Marina Halak

Printed in Malaysia

24 25 26 27 28   COS   10 9 8 7 6 5 4 3 2 1

Mfr: COS / Johor, Malaysia / August 2024 / PO #12232770

For Annie, Sophie, and Katie.
I love being your mama!

DAY 1
HOW TO HOPE

May the God of hope fill you with all joy and peace as you trust in him, so that you may overflow with hope by the power of the Holy Spirit.
ROMANS 15:13 NIV

Do you know what it means to hope for something? You probably use the word *hope* to say things like "I hope we go to Grandma's house tomorrow," or "I hope I get that new game for Christmas!" Usually we use the word *hope* when we want something to happen but we're not sure if it really *will* happen.

The Bible talks about hope too. But it's a little different.

The hope we see in God's Word *expects* something good will happen. This kind of hope is confident. You just know what you believe will come true! We can have this kind of hope when we trust in God because He can do anything.

That's what Advent is about—remembering the hope we have in God as we get ready to celebrate the birth of our hope-giving Savior, Jesus! Advent is a season to think about and praise God for the awesome things He offers us, like His love, peace, joy, and—you guessed it—hope!

READ ABOUT IT

Isaiah 7:14 NLT

The Lord himself will give you the sign. Look! The virgin will conceive a child! She will give birth to a son and will call him Immanuel (which means "God is with us").

TALK ABOUT IT

- What's something you're hoping for?
- How is that hope different from hoping in Jesus?
- What are you excited about during this Advent season?

GO ABOUT IT

Celebrate the start of Advent season as a family. Make a hot cocoa stand in your home with different flavors and toppings.

1. Find a space where you can set out your cocoa toppings.
2. Gather marshmallows, candy canes, chocolate chips, or whatever sounds yummy to you. Set them out in the space.
3. Ask a grown-up to help you make the hot cocoa (because this drink will be *hot*!).
4. Light a candle as you sip and thank God for the hope He offers.

PRAY ABOUT IT

Dear God, thank You for loving me and sending Jesus to earth for me. Please help me always put my hope in You. Amen.

LIGHT UP THE DARKNESS

The people who walk in darkness will see a great light.
ISAIAH 9:2 NLT

Imagine you're all alone walking through the shadowy woods at night. Scary, right? You'd probably feel better if you had a flashlight. (Or maybe even a lightsaber!) You'd want *something* to light your way.

Before God created the world, darkness was everywhere. But when God spoke on the first day of creation, light came beaming in. God saw that the light was good, and He continued creating for five more days. He made things like the land and seas, the fish and birds, animals of all kinds, and even humans. Everything God made was good. And on the seventh day, He rested.

There would be ups and downs in this new world–a lot like our own lives. But even when we feel sad or scared or alone, we can have hope because God is always here. He'll light up our darkness and beam His goodness into the hard moments. And even at the beginning of the world, God had a plan to bring another Light into the world–the One we're celebrating in Advent season right now. The Bible calls Jesus the Light of the World (John 8:12)!

READ ABOUT IT

Genesis 1:1–5 NIV

In the beginning God created the heavens and the earth. Now the earth was formless and empty, darkness was over the surface of the deep, and the Spirit of God was hovering over the waters. And God said, "Let there be light," and there was light. God saw that the light was good, and he separated the light from the darkness. God called the light "day," and the darkness he called "night."

You can keep reading about the Creation story in the rest of Genesis 1 and 2.

TALK ABOUT IT

- What are you afraid of? How could you trust God with that fear?
- What is one of your favorite parts of God's creation?
- Who is the Light who points everyone to God?

GO ABOUT IT

Have a flashlight dance party.

1. Find a flashlight (or two, or three).
2. Turn on your favorite Christmas music.
3. Shut off the lights, except for your flashlights.
4. Shine your flashlights all around as you move and groove!

EXTRA CHALLENGE: Take turns making spotlights for dance solos, and cheer each other on as you break it down.

PRAY ABOUT IT

Dear God, thank You for giving us a world filled with light and goodness and wonder. Help me remember that You are here for me, even when things are hard. Amen.

DAY 3
WE ALL FALL DOWN

So one man's sin brought guilt to all people. In the same way, one right act made people right with God.
ROMANS 5:18 NIrV

Have you ever done something you knew was wrong, even as you were doing it? Maybe you took an extra Christmas cookie when you were only supposed to have one. Or maybe you said something unkind or threw a snowball really hard at someone's face because you were mad at them. These wrong actions are called sins. Everyone sins and makes mistakes sometimes, even our favorite people.

Everything God made in creation was good and perfect. But the people He created made a very bad choice. The first people, Adam and Eve, thought they knew better than God, so they didn't listen to His instructions. And with one bite of fruit from a forbidden tree, the first sin happened.

Our sin separates us from God, which is a really sad thing. Sin lives in the darkness, in secret. But God wants us to live in His light, remember? That means living with honesty and goodness. Thankfully, God had an amazing plan to rescue people from the sadness that sin causes. His plan was Jesus! Because of Jesus, the entire world—including *you*—is able to be close to God through His forgiveness and love.

READ ABOUT IT

Genesis 3:2–6 NIV

The woman said to the serpent, "We may eat fruit from the trees in the garden, but God did say, 'You must not eat fruit from the tree that is in the middle of the garden, and you must not touch it, or you will die.'"

"You will not certainly die," the serpent said to the woman. "For God knows that when you eat from it your eyes will be opened, and you will be like God, knowing good and evil." . . .

She took some and ate it.

TALK ABOUT IT

- What's a bad choice you've made recently?
- Have you asked for forgiveness?
- Jesus did one thing so that we could be forgiven. Do you know what that one thing is?

PRAY ABOUT IT

Dear God, thank You for sending Your Son, Jesus, so that we could be forgiven. Thank You for loving me no matter what. Amen.

GO ABOUT IT

Make a homemade ornament that will remind you of God's love and forgiveness.

1. Gather a sheet of paper, a pair of scissors, a ribbon or string, and your favorite coloring supplies.
2. Cut out a heart shape from the paper. (Or come up with your own shape.)
3. Use the art supplies to decorate your shape. Be as creative or as simple as you want.
4. Have a grown-up help you make a hole at the top of the heart and thread the ribbon through it.
5. Tie the ribbon into a loop and find a special place to hang your new ornament.

A FAMILY TREE

But to all who believed him and accepted him, he gave the right to become children of God.
JOHN 1:12 NLT

This time of year, we see lots of Christmas trees covered with bright, twinkling lights. But have you ever seen a *family* tree? A family tree is a chart that shows family relationships, like moms, dads, siblings, and grandparents. Can you guess what this chart is shaped like? If you thought *a tree*, then you're right!

Jesus had lots of interesting people in His family tree. Let's start with a guy named Abraham. He was almost a hundred years old when God promised that he and his wife, Sarah, would have a baby. In fact, God said the whole world would be blessed because of Abraham's children and grandchildren and great-grandchildren and great-*great*-grandchildren—you get the idea. God certainly kept His promise to Abraham, because what could be a better blessing than eventually getting Jesus in his family tree?

Some of Jesus' other great-great-great (plus many more "greats") grandparents were kings and royalty. Others were just regular people who probably didn't seem special at all. But of course they were special—God chose them to be in Jesus' family.

And guess what? You can be part of Jesus' family too! When you choose to love and follow Jesus, you become one of God's children. Now that's something worth celebrating this Christmas!

READ ABOUT IT

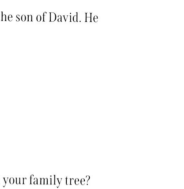

Matthew 1:1 NIrV

This is the written story of the family line of Jesus the Messiah. He is the son of David. He is also the son of Abraham.

   To read through Jesus' entire family tree, read Matthew 1:1–16.

TALK ABOUT IT

- Who are some of the people in your family tree?
- Why do you think God gives us families?
- How do you feel knowing that you can be part of Jesus' family?

GO ABOUT IT

Make your own family tree.

1. Gather a sheet of paper and some crayons or colored pencils.
2. Draw a tree on the paper with lots of branches.
3. Have an adult in your family help you write the names of family members.

EXTRA CHALLENGE: Choose someone from your family to call and tell about Jesus' family tree. Ask that person to tell you something about your own family that you might not know yet!

PRAY ABOUT IT

Dear God, thank You for giving me a wonderful family and for inviting me to be part of Your family too! I love being Your child. Amen.

DAY 5
BEFORE THE BIRTH

> The Lord himself will give you a sign. The virgin is going to have a baby. She will give birth to a son. And he will be called Immanuel.
>
> **ISAIAH 7:14 NIrV**

Before you were born, many people were so excited for you to come into the world: your parents, the doctors and nurses who helped deliver you, and other friends and family members. They had been waiting for months to meet you! But did you know that people had been talking about Jesus for *hundreds* of years before He was born? Talk about a long wait!

In the Old Testament we can read about many prophets and prophecies. A *prophet* is someone who gets a message from God, and the message they get is called a *prophecy*. Prophets share those prophecies from God with others. Many of these messages in the Old Testament were about the coming Savior. In fact, over three hundred prophecies about Jesus have already come true!

One prophet named Isaiah shared many prophecies about Jesus. Isaiah knew that Jesus would be amazing, and he told people to be on the lookout for Him. It would be many, many years before Jesus would come to earth, but it didn't matter. People were already so excited about this wonderful, mighty, everlasting Leader!

READ ABOUT IT

Isaiah 9:6 NIV

For to us a child is born,
to us a son is given,
and the government will be on his shoulders.
And he will be called
Wonderful Counselor, Mighty God,
Everlasting Father, Prince of Peace.

TALK ABOUT IT

- What's something that makes you excited every time you think about it?
- What were some of the names Isaiah used to describe Jesus? What do they mean?
- Why do you think people were *so* excited about Jesus?

GO ABOUT IT

Prepare for a delicious meal as you make plans for a happy Advent season.

1. Have a grown-up in your family write down everyone's favorite meal on separate pieces of paper. Put them in a hat or bowl and draw to see whose dinner "wins."
2. Help your grown-up gather the ingredients to make the meal. For some extra razzle dazzle, try making a meal with a red and green color theme!
3. Find ways to make it feel like an adventure as you cook together, like maybe pretending you are chefs working in a big, fancy restaurant.
4. While you eat the meal, ask each family member to share one thing they'd like to do together during Advent season.

EXTRA CHALLENGE: Repeat steps 1–3 to make a yummy dessert!

PRAY ABOUT IT

Dear God, thank You for always doing what You promise, including sending Jesus! Help me to keep learning about how wonderful and mighty Jesus truly is. Amen.

DAY 6
WAITING FOR A SAVIOR

Yet those who wait for the Lord
Will gain new strength;
They will mount up with wings like eagles,
They will run and not get tired,
They will walk and not become weary.
ISAIAH 40:31 NASB

How do you feel when you need to wait a long time for something? At school, you have to stand in line for your turn on the slide, don't you? Maybe you have to wait for the city bus to take you to your friend's house. Maybe you've been waiting for Christmas to come, and it seems like it's taking *forever*. Sometimes it seems like all you do is wait, wait, and wait some more.

But how would you feel if you had to wait *four hundred years* for one of those things? That would be pretty hard, right?

Not long after the story of Daniel and the lions' den, God seemed to go quiet. Four hundred years went by before God's people, the Israelites, heard from Him again. But the good news is, the next time they received a message from Him, God was bringing Jesus into the world.

Those four hundred years weren't easy for God's people. In fact, some gave up hope in hearing from God ever again and gave in to behaving like the unbelievers around them instead of like God followers. But others kept waiting and hoping that one day their Savior would come. And He did!

READ ABOUT IT

Malachi 3:1 NIV

"I will send my messenger, who will prepare the way before me. Then suddenly the Lord you are seeking will come to his temple; the messenger of the covenant, whom you desire, will come," says the LORD Almighty.

TALK ABOUT IT

- Have you ever had to wait a long time for something? What was it?
- Why do you think it's hard to wait?
- How do you think it would have felt waiting for Jesus to come?

GO ABOUT IT

Play a waiting game!

1. Lay out a blanket in a cozy spot in your home, such as in front of the Christmas tree.
2. Pick out a game where each player needs to wait for their turn. This could be a board game, I Spy, Charades, or another game you enjoy.
3. As you wait for your turn, try your best to be patient. Remember, God's people waited hundreds of years for Jesus—you can wait for a few minutes!

Dear God, thank You for sending Jesus after such a long time of waiting. Please help me to practice patience whenever I need to wait. Amen.

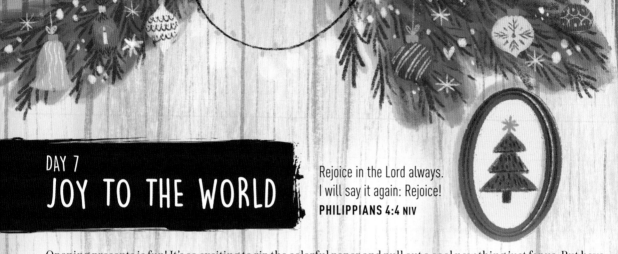

DAY 7
JOY TO THE WORLD

Rejoice in the Lord always.
I will say it again: Rejoice!
PHILIPPIANS 4:4 NIV

Opening presents is fun! It's so exciting to rip the colorful paper and pull out a cool new thing just for us. But have you ever gotten bored with a favorite present after a week, or maybe even a day? The new toy or game or pair of shoes doesn't make you happy anymore.

There are a lot of things that make us feel joyful for a little while. But the joy that we sing about in the song "Joy to the World" is different. Real joy doesn't depend on what fun (or not-so-fun) things we're doing that day or how many presents are underneath the Christmas tree. This kind of joy comes from knowing that God loves us and that He sent Jesus for us.

Be joyful as you celebrate what Christmas is all about–that Jesus came to earth to show us His love. And this special joy isn't only for Christmastime–we can enjoy it all year long!

READ ABOUT IT

1 Peter 1:6–9 NLT

So be truly glad. There is wonderful joy ahead, even though you must endure many trials for a little while.... So when your faith remains strong through many trials, it will bring you much praise and glory and honor on the day when Jesus Christ is revealed to the whole world. You love him even though you have never seen him. Though you do not see him now, you trust him; and you rejoice with a glorious, inexpressible joy. The reward for trusting him will be the salvation of your souls.

TALK ABOUT IT

- What are some things that make you feel joyful?
- Why is Jesus' birth so exciting?
- How is joy from Jesus different from the feeling you have when you open a gift?

GO ABOUT IT

Celebrate the second week of Advent as a family.

1. With an adult's help, light two candles.
2. Read the lyrics to the song "Joy to the World."
3. Come up with actions or simple dance moves to go along with the lyrics.
4. Sing the song and do the actions together.

PRAY ABOUT IT

Dear God, thank You for Your joy that
lasts all year long. Help me find real joy
from knowing Jesus. Amen.

DAY 8
AN UNEXPECTED VISITOR

The angel went to her and said, "Greetings, you who are highly favored! The Lord is with you."
LUKE 1:28 NIV

Imagine you're eating a snack at the kitchen table when someone suddenly appears right in front of you. He is dressed in the brightest white you've ever seen. And then he starts telling you something that sounds too crazy and too amazing to be true. You would probably think you were dreaming, right?

That's what happened to Mary. And it was no dream. A *real* angel named Gabriel came to her in *real* life! At first she was afraid, and who could blame her? Not only did Gabriel just show up, but he told Mary that she would give birth to the Son of God.

Wait, *what?*

This was all quite confusing to Mary. It didn't seem possible that she could have a baby—she wasn't even married yet. But the angel explained this baby would be born from God's Spirit and that God can do anything.

Mary was probably still shocked and a little confused, but she believed Gabriel anyway. "I am the Lord's servant," Mary answered. "May your word to me be fulfilled."

READ ABOUT IT

Luke 1:28–33 NIV

The angel went to her and said, "Greetings, you who are highly favored! The Lord is with you."

Mary was greatly troubled at his words and wondered what kind of greeting this might be. But the angel said to her, "Do not be afraid, Mary; you have found favor with God. You will conceive and give birth to a son, and you are to call him Jesus. He will be great and will be called the Son of the Most High. The Lord God will give him the throne of his father David, and . . . his kingdom will never end."

GO ABOUT IT

Surprise someone with an invitation for a special Christmas event!

1. Decide what (and who) your invitation will be for. The invitation could be asking someone to come to church with you for a Christmas service, or it could be for a gathering to celebrate the birth of Jesus together.
2. Grab a sheet of paper, coloring supplies, and anything else you might want to create a festive Christmas invitation.
3. Send or give the invitation to whoever you have in mind!

TALK ABOUT IT

- Have you ever had a surprise visitor?
- What did Gabriel say about Mary's baby?
- Who could you tell about the big news of Jesus coming to earth?

PRAY ABOUT IT

Dear God, thank You for sending Your very own Son to earth for me. Please fill me up with excitement instead of fear this Advent season. Amen.

DAY 9
SHARE YOUR JOY

"Now I am coming to you. I told them many things while I was with them in this world so they would be filled with my joy."
JOHN 17:13 NLT

Has something big and exciting ever happened to you? Maybe you got an invitation to your best friend's birthday party or learned how to ride a two-wheel bike. Or maybe you found out you were going to be a big brother or sister!

When something exciting happens, what do you do? Do you jump around, spin, and somersault? Do you do a happy dance? Maybe you do all the above! But *then* what do you do? You're probably so happy that you have to go tell someone!

That's exactly what Mary did after learning she would give birth to the Son of God. Can you imagine how excited she felt? What a big, crazy, amazing thing to share! So Mary hurried to find her cousin Elizabeth, and she told her all about what had happened. Elizabeth was pregnant too, and when the baby in her belly heard Mary's greeting, he jumped with joy!

READ ABOUT IT

Luke 1:41–45 NIrV

When Elizabeth heard Mary's greeting, the baby inside her jumped. And Elizabeth was filled with the Holy Spirit. In a loud voice she called out, "God has blessed you more than other women. And blessed is the child you will have! . . . As soon as I heard the sound of your voice, the baby inside me jumped for joy. You are a woman God has blessed. You have believed that the Lord would keep his promises to you!"

TALK ABOUT IT

- What is exciting news you've told someone recently?
- Why does knowing about Jesus bring you joy?
- How can you share Jesus' joy with the people around you?

PRAY ABOUT IT

Dear God, thank You for sending Jesus to earth to be our Savior. Please help me share Your joy with others. Amen.

GO ABOUT IT

Share some joy with the people around you.

1. Give extra friendly smiles to the people you pass by.
2. Call a family member and sing them a Christmas carol.
3. Tell someone about how much Jesus loves them!

DAY 10
MARY'S SONG

"My soul glorifies the Lord and my spirit rejoices in God my Savior."
LUKE 1:46–47 NIV

Do you have a favorite Christmas song? Maybe you love singing "Away in a Manger" or "Silent Night." It can be hard to choose a favorite because there are many wonderful songs about Jesus' birth. But did you know that Mary, Jesus' mom, wrote her own song?

When Mary visited her cousin Elizabeth and told her about Jesus, she was filled with joy and gratitude. Then she said some beautiful words that are often called "The Magnificat" or "Mary's Song." Now, Mary may not have sung these words to a tune or melody, but maybe she did. Either way, her words show a beautiful picture of the excitement she felt knowing that Jesus would be born—and that she was the one chosen to be His mother!

As you sing songs this Christmas, remember Mary and try to sing with the same joy and excitement she had all those years ago.

READ ABOUT IT

Luke 1:46–50 NIV

And Mary said:

"My soul glorifies the Lord
and my spirit rejoices in God my Savior,
for he has been mindful
of the humble state of his servant.
From now on all generations will call me blessed,
for the Mighty One has done great things for me—
holy is his name.
His mercy extends to those who fear him,
from generation to generation."

Read the rest of Mary's Song in Luke 1:51–55.

GO ABOUT IT

Lift up your voice and share the joy of music.

1. Have everyone in your family pick out one (or more) of their favorite Christmas songs about Jesus.
2. Practice the songs together.
3. Go caroling! You can do traditional caroling by going door to door as a group, or you can hop on a video call and bring some joy to relatives far away.

TALK ABOUT IT

- Do you like to sing?
- If you could sing only one Christmas song all December long, what would it be?
- Why do we sing songs about Jesus' birth at Christmastime?

PRAY ABOUT IT

Dear God, thank You for blessing my life with beautiful music. Help me praise You with my thoughts, words, and songs today and every day. Amen.

DAY 11
THE WHOLE STORY

A joyful heart makes a cheerful face, but when the heart is sad, the spirit is broken.
PROVERBS 15:13 NASB

Have you ever heard something that made you sad? Or glad? Or mad? How about just really confused? We all experience different emotions every day. Sometimes we have so many big feelings, it's like we're on a roller coaster: up and down, up and down.

Joseph probably felt all sorts of emotions when he heard Mary was pregnant. You see, Joseph was engaged to be married to Mary. But they weren't married yet, so he didn't understand how she was going to have a baby *now*. He didn't know this baby belonged to God. He probably felt sad and hurt, and he decided that he wouldn't marry her after all.

Thankfully, an angel came to visit Joseph in a dream. The angel explained to Joseph that the baby was God's Son! *Wow.* Joseph believed the angel and did what the angel told him: he married Mary and named the baby Jesus.

Can you imagine how Joseph might have felt after finding out the full story? Talk about a roller coaster! His emotions probably shot up from sad and mad to happy and glad. Emotions can help us make decisions about our lives, but they can also mislead us. We always need to check our emotions with the truth and get the whole story before we act on how we feel.

READ ABOUT IT

Matthew 1:20–21 NIrV

But as Joseph was thinking about this, an angel of the Lord appeared to him in a dream. The angel said, "Joseph, son of David, don't be afraid to take Mary home as your wife. The baby inside her is from the Holy Spirit. She is going to have a son. You must give him the name Jesus. That's because he will save his people from their sins."

Read the rest of the story in Matthew 1:18–24.

TALK ABOUT IT

- What emotions are you feeling right now?
- Have you ever been upset about something but felt differently after hearing the full story?
- Why do you think God gives us emotions?

GO ABOUT IT

Explore your favorite Christmas stories.

1. Pick out a few of your favorite Christmas books.
2. Get cozy and read the books together as a family.
3. Talk about the emotions the characters feel throughout the stories.

EXTRA CHALLENGE: What would happen if the writer stopped writing mid-story? Would you have written a different ending? Talk together about how you would have ended these stories.

PRAY ABOUT IT

Dear God, thank You for making us with feelings that tell us so much about ourselves and our world. Help me trust You and look for truth, no matter what I'm feeling. Amen.

DAY 12
A LONG JOURNEY (TO BETHLEHEM)

"But you, Bethlehem Ephrathah, though you are small among the clans of Judah, out of you will come for me one who will be ruler over Israel, whose origins are from of old, from ancient times."
MICAH 5:2 NIV

Imagine you're getting ready for a long trip. What would you bring along? Maybe extra clothes, a blanket, a few books, and some soap. (You don't want to be smelly, right?!) But then, when you're finally packed and it's time to load up, there's no car or bus or plane. Nope. You lace up your sandals and get ready to walk. (Maybe you'll get to ride a donkey if you need a break!)

Before Jesus was born, Mary and Joseph found out they needed to go to Bethlehem, the town Joseph was from. Bethlehem was about ninety miles from where Mary and Joseph lived in Nazareth, and they had to walk to get there. Their journey probably took them about a week, but it might've taken longer because Mary was about to have a baby. She likely needed extra breaks to rest her tired feet.

This journey was important to God's plans. Hundreds of years before Mary and Joseph's trip, a prophet named Micah told God's people that the Messiah, Jesus, would come from the little, unimpressive town of Bethlehem! How cool is that?!

READ ABOUT IT

Luke 2:4–5 NIV

So Joseph also went up from the town of Nazareth in Galilee to Judea, to Bethlehem the town of David, because he belonged to the house and line of David. He went there . . . with Mary, who was pledged to be married to him and was expecting a child.

TALK ABOUT IT

- What's the name of the town where Mary and Joseph traveled?
- What's the farthest you've ever traveled? If you walked there, how long do you think the journey would take?
- Why might God want us to go to different places?

GO ABOUT IT

Take your own winter journey.

1. Choose a place your family can travel to, like the park, your grandma's house, or the library.
2. Figure out what you'll need for your trip and pack those items. Do you need snacks, warm winter gear, or some kind of vehicle?
3. Enjoy your journey together!

EXTRA CHALLENGE: Draw a map of your journey.

PRAY ABOUT IT

Dear God, thank You for being with me no matter where I am in the world. Please show me the places where You want me to go. Amen.

DAY 13
THE PRESENT OF PEACE

"Peace I leave with you; my peace I give you. I do not give to you as the world gives. Do not let your hearts be troubled and do not be afraid."
JOHN 14:27 NIV

What scares you? Do you shake at the thought of giant spiders, sharp-toothed sharks, or even imaginary monsters under your bed? We've all felt afraid or worried, and it's no fun. But the Bible has good news!

God wants to give us peace. The prophet Isaiah called Jesus the Prince of Peace (Isaiah 9:6). So if Prince Jesus is in charge of your life, you don't have to sit around and worry all day. (Because who wants to do *that*?) You can have peace because He will take care of you.

Having peace means feeling calm and believing that everything is going to be all right. We can have peace in our relationships when we get along with our siblings. We can also have peace in our hearts, which helps us not to worry.

When we follow Jesus and trust in Him, we can have the *best* kind of peace. We can rest and relax and not be afraid of the scary things in this world. Sure, things might still feel frightening at times, but Jesus is bigger and stronger than whatever we're worried about. He gives us a powerful peace that lasts forever.

READ ABOUT IT

Mark 4:35, 37–39 NIrV

When evening came, Jesus said to his disciples, "Let's go over to the other side of the lake." . . . A wild storm came up. Waves crashed over the boat. It was about to sink. Jesus was in the back, sleeping on a cushion. The disciples woke him up. They said, "Teacher! Don't you care if we drown?"

He got up and ordered the wind to stop. He said to the waves, "Quiet! Be still!" Then the wind died down. And it was completely calm.

TALK ABOUT IT

- What were the disciples afraid of in the Bible story?
- What are things you can do to remind yourself that Jesus is bigger than your fears?
- The next time you're feeling afraid, how can you trade worry for peace?

GO ABOUT IT

Celebrate the third week of Advent as a family.

1. With an adult's help, light three candles.
2. Find a cozy, peaceful spot where you can sit together.
3. Take turns sharing what you're nervous about for the coming week. Then, talk about what you're looking forward to this week.
4. Pray together, and hand over your worries to Jesus.

PRAY ABOUT IT

Dear God, thank You for being bigger and stronger than whatever makes me afraid. Please help me to have the gift of peace that comes from Jesus. Amen.

DAY 14
AWAY IN A MANGER

She wrapped him in cloths and placed him in a manger, because there was no guest room available for them.
LUKE 2:7 NIV

When a future king is born, how do you think people prepare for him? They make sure the room is warm and filled with the finest things, including soft, clean blankets. But for the King of all kings, things looked a *little* different.

When Mary and Joseph got to Bethlehem, there were no guest rooms left for them. So they stayed where animals were kept, maybe in a cave or a stable—we don't know exactly. What we do know is that after Jesus was born, He was placed in a manger. Just in case you're thinking a manger is a cute old-timey crib for babies, it's not. A manger is something animals eat from. Jesus, the Savior of the world, was laid in a feeding box for animals like cows and donkeys!

So why was Jesus born in such a plain, smelly place? Because God wanted to show us that Jesus came for everyone! He didn't come for just rich or famous or popular people. He came for *all* people. He came for you and for me.

READ ABOUT IT

Luke 2:6–7 NIV

While they were there, the time came for the baby to be born, and she gave birth to her firstborn, a son. She wrapped him in cloths and placed him in a manger, because there was no guest room available for them.

TALK ABOUT IT

- Who did Jesus come to earth for?
- What kind of animals do you think were there when Jesus was born?
- How could you help someone learn that Jesus loves everyone, including them?

GO ABOUT IT

Act out the nativity story.

1. Make a fort with chairs and blankets–this will be your stable.
2. Grab stuffed animals and a laundry basket for a manger. Place them inside the stable.
3. Assign people to play the characters, such as Mary, Joseph, an innkeeper, and a donkey.
4. Act out the story with scenes such as traveling to Bethlehem, looking for a place to stay, and Jesus being laid in a manger.

PRAY ABOUT IT

Dear God, thank You for sending Jesus to earth for everyone, including me. Help me to show Jesus' love to others this Christmas. Amen.

DAY 15
THE GREATEST GIFT

Let us give thanks to God for his gift. It is so great that no one can tell how wonderful it really is!
2 CORINTHIANS 9:15 NIrV

How do you feel when you see a big box wrapped in shiny paper with your name on the tag? You're probably pretty excited, right? Getting presents can be fun, but the best gift in the world doesn't fit under a Christmas tree. Nope. Because the best gift ever is Jesus!

Presents can break or become lost. Your new favorite shirt gets stained. The toy you had to have gets eaten by the vacuum cleaner. But Jesus is a gift that lasts forever. When you follow Jesus, He will be with you here on earth and then in heaven.

There is no present under a tree that can compare to God's gift of Jesus. God knew that His people needed this gift back then, and He knew we would still need this gift today. God performed the miracle of sending baby Jesus because He loves you so much. He sent Jesus to save you because He wants to be close to you now and forever.

READ ABOUT IT

John 1:14, 16–17 NLT

So the Word became human and made his home among us. He was full of unfailing love and faithfulness. And we have seen his glory, the glory of the Father's one and only Son. . . .

From his abundance we have all received one gracious blessing after another. For the law was given through Moses, but God's unfailing love and faithfulness came through Jesus Christ.

GO ABOUT IT

Make your old gifts last longer by sharing them.

1. Go through your toys and choose some you could donate to others.
2. Have a grown-up help you find an organization that accepts gently used toys.
3. Pray for the kids who will get your toys. Ask God to help them know that Jesus is the greatest gift ever.

EXTRA CHALLENGE: Buy items for an Angel Tree family, or pick out gifts for families in other parts of the world through an organization like Compassion International or Samaritan's Purse.

TALK ABOUT IT

- What is your favorite present you've ever received at Christmas?
- What is your favorite present that you've given someone else?
- Why is Jesus better than any present we could get or give?

Dear God, thank You for giving us Jesus. Help me remember that He is the greatest gift I could ever receive. Amen.

DAY 16
ANGELS HEARD ON HIGH

Let everything that has breath praise the Lord. Praise the Lord.
PSALM 150:6 NIV

When you picture an angel, what do you see? Maybe you imagine a kind lady wearing white clothes with a halo on top of her head. While we don't know exactly what angels look like, we do know that when they show themselves to humans in the Bible, those humans usually seem pretty scared at first.

This is definitely how a group of shepherds felt when an angel appeared to them one night in a field. They were minding their own business and watching over their sheep, when an angel suddenly showed up. The Bible says the shepherds were terrified. But the angel quickly told them not to be afraid. This heavenly messenger had exciting news!

The angel told the shepherds that the Savior had been born and they could find the special baby lying in a manger. After that, an entire group of angels appeared! It's a good thing they didn't all show up at first—imagine how scared the shepherds would have been seeing an *army* of angels before hearing the great news about Jesus. This angel army wasn't there to battle, though—they were there to praise God!

READ ABOUT IT

Luke 2:8–14 NIV

And there were shepherds living out in the fields nearby, keeping watch over their flocks at night. An angel of the Lord appeared to them, and the glory of the Lord shone around them, and they were terrified. But the angel said to them, "Do not be afraid. I bring you good news that will cause great joy for all the people. Today in the town of David a Savior has been born to you; he is the Messiah, the Lord. This will be a sign to you: You will find a baby wrapped in cloths and lying in a manger."

Suddenly a great company of the heavenly host appeared with the angel, praising God and saying,

"Glory to God in the highest heaven."

TALK ABOUT IT

- What did the angel say to the shepherds?
- Why does God deserve our praise and worship?
- What are some ways that you can praise God?

GO ABOUT IT

Make a praise poster.

1. Get a large poster board, or tape four sheets of paper together to make your own "poster."
2. Gather coloring supplies and stickers.
3. Decorate the poster board with things you want to praise God for during Advent season. Maybe you want to praise Him for His love, for making the beautiful stars, or for sending Jesus!
4. Find a place to hang the poster, and praise God whenever you see it.

PRAY ABOUT IT

Dear God, thank You for being so good and choosing to send Jesus. You deserve all our praise! Amen.

DAY 17
THE SHEPHERDS' VISIT

He will feed his flock like a shepherd. He will carry the lambs in his arms, holding them close to his heart.
ISAIAH 40:11 NLT

Do you know what a shepherd's job is? They care for sheep! Being a shepherd isn't a fancy job, but sheep need someone to lead them and watch over them. Sheep don't do well on their own.

After the shepherds near Bethlehem were visited by the angels, they knew they wanted to see this special baby. They hurried to find Jesus, the Savior, wrapped in cloths and lying in a trough meant to hold food for animals.

The angels could have gone to kings and queens or other important leaders to announce Jesus' birth. But instead, they went to some ordinary people who were just doing their daily work. Why did the angels do this? Maybe to show that Jesus came for all people—both the fancy and the not-so-fancy. The angels also might have gone to the shepherds because after Jesus grew up, He talked about Himself as "the Good Shepherd." Jesus will lovingly lead anyone who will follow Him, much like a shepherd leads his flock!

Even if people didn't think being a shepherd was a very important job, God knew this wasn't true. God sent His Son to earth to be the perfect Shepherd who will protect, lead, and love us forever!

READ ABOUT IT

Luke 2:15–16 NIrV

The angels left and went into heaven. Then the shepherds said to one another, "Let's go to Bethlehem. Let's see this thing that has happened, which the Lord has told us about."

So they hurried off and found Mary and Joseph and the baby. The baby was lying in the manger.

TALK ABOUT IT

- Do you think you would enjoy working as a shepherd? Why or why not?
- Who is the Good Shepherd?
- What are some ways that Jesus leads His sheep? (*Psst,* that's us!)

GO ABOUT IT

Play "Follow the Shepherd."

1. Choose someone to be the shepherd.
2. Line up behind the shepherd and follow that person around while copying their movements and actions.
3. Take turns being the shepherd until everyone has had a chance to lead.

EXTRA CHALLENGE: Dress up in fun or silly Christmas outfits before you play! You could wear ugly Christmas sweaters, Christmas pajamas, or other Christmas-y items you have around.

PRAY ABOUT IT

Dear God, thank You for Jesus, our Good Shepherd, who wants to lead us. Help me choose to love and follow Him. Amen.

DAY 18
SPREAD THE NEWS

He said to them, "Go into all the world. Preach the good news to everyone."
MARK 16:15 NIrV

What kinds of news do you like to share with others? Do you tell your parents about what you did at school? Do you talk to your friends about your favorite movies or games? We can share all sorts of things with people, but the most important thing we could ever tell someone about is Jesus' love for them!

When the shepherds saw baby Jesus, they knew He was special. They were so excited that they *had* to tell others about Him! Everyone who heard about Jesus was amazed by what the shepherds said—God's Rescuer whom they had been waiting for had finally come!

The shepherds are a great example of how we can spread the news about Jesus. Advent is a wonderful time of year to talk to someone about Him because He's the reason we celebrate Christmas in the first place. You might know this truth, but your neighbor, family member, or friend from school might not. You could be the one to tell them the amazing news that God loves them and sent Jesus for them!

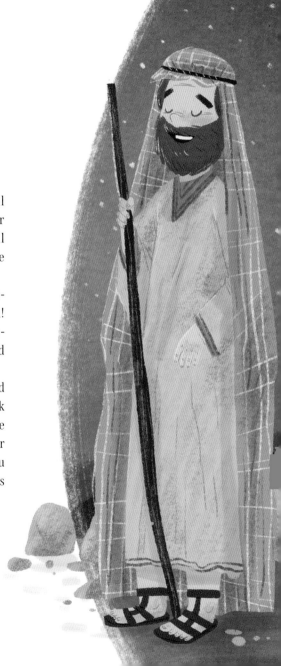

READ ABOUT IT

Luke 2:17–20 NIrV

After the shepherds had seen him, they told everyone. They reported what the angel had said about this child. All who heard it were amazed at what the shepherds said to them. But Mary kept all these things like a secret treasure in her heart. She thought about them over and over. The shepherds returned. They gave glory and praise to God. Everything they had seen and heard was just as they had been told.

TALK ABOUT IT

- What's the best news you've ever heard?
- Have you ever told someone about Jesus?
- Who could you tell the story of Jesus' birth to this Christmas?

GO ABOUT IT

Spread some holiday sweetness.

1. Close your eyes and think of your *favorite* Christmas cookie.
2. With a grown-up, gather the ingredients and bake those cookies. Or pick out some delicious-looking cookies from the store.
3. Give the cookies to your neighbors and wish them a Merry Christmas.

EXTRA CHALLENGE: Decorate a box or bag to put the cookies in, and include a kind note with a Bible verse.

PRAY ABOUT IT

Dear God, thank You for the shepherds' example of how we can spread the news about Jesus' birth. Help me to tell others about Jesus too! Amen.

DAY 19
SENT TO LOVE

"For God so loved the world that he gave his one and only Son, that whoever believes in him shall not perish but have eternal life."
JOHN 3:16 NIV

Do you ever say things like, "I love macaroni and cheese," "I love swimming," or "I love dressing my dog in funny outfits"? People use the word *love* for a lot of things. But God's love for us is way bigger than how you feel when you eat gooey cheese or top your puppy with a hat. Our favorite foods and activities change over time, but God's love is always here.

God gives us a never-ending, forever-and-always kind of love. He never wakes up and says, "I don't feel like loving this person today." His love doesn't change based on what you do, and He loves you more than you can even imagine. Isn't that amazing? The same God who made the sun and the stars loves you like crazy!

God loves you so much that He sent Jesus, His one and only Son, to earth to rescue you from sin. He did this even though He knew that one day Jesus would have to die on a cross. But when Jesus did that, He took the punishment for the sins of anyone who would follow Him so that they could be with Him forever. Now that's real love!

READ ABOUT IT

Romans 8:38–39 NIrV

I am absolutely sure that not even death or life can separate us from God's love. Not even angels or demons . . . the highest places or the lowest, or anything else in all creation can separate us. Nothing at all can separate us from God's love. That's because of what Jesus Christ our Lord has done.

TALK ABOUT IT

- What are some things you like a lot?
- How would you describe God's love?
- How can you love others the way God loves you?

GO ABOUT IT

Celebrate the fourth week of Advent as a family.

1. With an adult's help, light four candles.
2. Pack a picnic-style meal and spread out a blanket in your favorite spot in your home.
3. Have an indoor picnic together! As you eat, talk about God's love and share ideas for showing God's love to others.

PRAY ABOUT IT

Dear God, thank You for loving me so much that You sent Jesus to die for me and save me. Help me choose to love others the way You love me. Amen.

DAY 20
A BIG PROMISE

So know that the Lord your God is God. He is the faithful God. He will keep his agreement of love for a thousand lifetimes. He does this for people who love him and obey his commands.
DEUTERONOMY 7:9 ICB

Has anyone ever told you they would do something, but then they didn't do it? It doesn't feel good when people break their promises. But do you know who never breaks a promise? God!

An old man named Simeon had loved and followed God his whole life. And God promised Simeon that he would see the Savior—the One who would rescue the world—before he died. After Jesus was born, Simeon went to the temple, a place people would go to praise and worship God. While he was there, he noticed Mary and Joseph and their small baby boy. He knew this baby was the King of all kings! He took Jesus in his arms and praised God for keeping His promise.

A prophet named Anna came up to join this small but important celebration. She was very old, and she loved and followed God like Simeon. Anna also understood that Jesus was the Savior. She thanked God and praised Him for sending this baby who would one day save us all!

READ ABOUT IT

Luke 2:25–28 NIrV

In Jerusalem there was a man named Simeon. He was a good and godly man. He was waiting for God's promise to Israel to come true. The Holy Spirit was with him. The Spirit had told Simeon that he would not die before he had seen the Lord's Messiah. The Spirit led him into the temple courtyard. Then Jesus' parents brought the child in. They came to do for him what the Law required. Simeon took Jesus in his arms and praised God.

TALK ABOUT IT

- Has someone ever broken a promise to you? Have you ever broken a promise?
- How do you feel knowing that God never breaks His promises?
- What are some promises God made to us?

GO ABOUT IT

Learn how to say "Merry Christmas" in different languages. Here are some to get you started!

- SPANISH: Feliz Navidad (feh-lees nah-bee-dahd)
- FRENCH: Joyeux Noël (zhua-yuh no-el)
- ITALIAN: Buon Natale (buon na-ta-leh)
- SWEDISH: God Jul (guhd juhl)
- KOREAN: 메리 크리스마스 (Meli Keuliseumaseu; mehr-lee kris-mus-uhr)

PRAY ABOUT IT

Dear God, thank You for always keeping Your promises. Help me to trust that You will always love me and never leave me. Amen.

DAY 21
A STAR IN THE SKY

Trust in the Lord with all your heart. Do not depend on your own understanding. In all your ways obey him. Then he will make your paths smooth and straight.
PROVERBS 3:5–6 NIrV

If you were going somewhere for the first time, how would you know how to get there? These days lots of people use technology, like Google Maps or GPS, to get from place to place. But back in Jesus' day, people didn't have cell phones or tablets. Can you imagine a life without *any* technology?

When Jesus was born, there was no internet to spread the news. There was no group chat or social media for Mary and Joseph to share a baby announcement. Instead, God placed a special star in the sky. This star signaled to some wise men that the new King had been born. The wise men decided to go and worship this small King, so they headed out on a long journey, following the star.

God guided the wise men to Jesus, and today He wants to guide all of us to know and follow Jesus too. God leads us with things like His Word, wise people who love Jesus, and the Holy Spirit, who lives inside everyone who believes that Jesus is the Savior!

READ ABOUT IT

Matthew 2:1–6 NLT

About that time some wise men from eastern lands arrived in Jerusalem, asking, "Where is the newborn king of the Jews? We saw his star as it rose, and we have come to worship him."

King Herod was deeply disturbed when he heard this, as was everyone in Jerusalem. He called a meeting of the leading priests and teachers of religious law and asked, "Where is the Messiah supposed to be born?"

"In Bethlehem in Judea," they said, "for this is what the prophet wrote:

'And you, O Bethlehem in the land of Judah,
are not least among the ruling cities of Judah,
for a ruler will come from you
who will be the shepherd for my people Israel.'"

GO ABOUT IT

Go stargazing.

1. Look at the weather forecast to find out when the next clear night will be.
2. Choose a place to stargaze from like a big window, porch, or yard. If you're not able to see many stars, have a grown-up help you find a stargazing website.
3. Enjoy this part of God's creation! You can look for constellations or certain stars in the sky that stand out.

EXTRA CHALLENGE: Try to find the Big Dipper and the Little Dipper. (Hint: They look like ladles.) Then try to find the North Star, which is at the end of the Little Dipper's handle. Explorers have used the North Star to navigate for thousands of years!

TALK ABOUT IT

- What would it be like to have no technology?
- What did the wise men follow to find Jesus?
- How does God guide us today?

PRAY ABOUT IT

Dear God, thank You for the things that guide me, like the Bible and Your Spirit. Help me to follow the paths You want me to take. Amen.

DAY 22
SOME VERY WISE MEN

If any of you needs wisdom, you should ask God for it. He will give it to you. God gives freely to everyone and doesn't find fault.
JAMES 1:5 NIrV

Did you know that in many Bible translations the wise men are called the magi? Some traditions even call them the three kings. But many people who study the Bible don't think they were actually kings or that there were only three of them. You've probably heard them most commonly called the Wise Men, but do you know why we call them wise?

We don't know a whole lot about them, but here's what we *do* know:

- They read God's Word.
- They were looking for Jesus.
- They knew Jesus was special.
- They brought meaningful gifts fit for a king.
- They kept Jesus safe by avoiding the evil king Herod on their way home.

Those are all smart things to do, so these were clearly some very wise men!

Would you call yourself wise? If you do anything on the list above, you are on your way to becoming a wise kid! God will give us wisdom if we ask Him for it. So this Christmas, try asking God for the gift of wisdom. He would love to give it to you.

READ ABOUT IT

Matthew 2:7–10 NIrV

Then Herod secretly called for the Wise Men. He found out from them exactly when the star had appeared. He sent them to Bethlehem. He said, "Go and search carefully for the child. As soon as you find him, report it to me. Then I can go and worship him too."

After the Wise Men had listened to the king, they went on their way. The star they had seen when it rose went ahead of them. It finally stopped over the place where the child was. When they saw the star, they were filled with joy.

TALK ABOUT IT

- What does it mean to be wise?
- Who are some wise people in your life?
- How can you continue to become wiser each day?

GO ABOUT IT

Play "Wise or Not Wise."

1. Pick out a favorite Christmas movie to watch together as a family.
2. Get some popcorn or another snack to enjoy as you watch.
3. Pause the movie after a character makes a decision. Talk about whether that character's decision was wise or not wise. (Grown-ups: If stopping and starting feels too distracting, jot down some of the characters' decisions on a sheet of paper so you can discuss them together after the movie is over.)

PRAY ABOUT IT

Dear God, thank You for offering me the gift of wisdom. Please help me to grow wiser by following Jesus each day. Amen.

DAY 23
GIFTS FOR THE KING

"In everything I did, I showed you that by this kind of hard work we must help the weak, remembering the words the Lord Jesus himself said: 'It is more blessed to give than to receive.'"
ACTS 20:35 NIV

Have you ever heard the saying "it's better to give than to receive"? This idea comes from something Jesus said that's recorded in the Bible.

Do you think Jesus was right? Do we really get more blessings when we give gifts instead of receiving them? Well, Jesus is God's perfect Son, so of course He was right!

In fact, current research and scientific studies say the exact same thing. We feel better, happier, and more joyful when we give to others than when we get something for ourselves. This doesn't mean that you can't enjoy getting presents. But if you aren't giving gifts to others, you are really missing out.

The wise men seemed to understand the importance of giving gifts because they brought very special gifts for Jesus—gold, frankincense, and myrrh. Can you say those out loud? *Gold*, *frankincense*, and *myrrh*. These generous gifts of a precious metal and expensive herbs and spices were surely fit for a king!

READ ABOUT IT

Matthew 2:11–12 NIrV

The Wise Men went to the house. There they saw the child with his mother Mary. They bowed down and worshiped him. Then they opened their treasures. They gave him gold, frankincense and myrrh. But God warned them in a dream not to go back to Herod. So they returned to their country on a different road.

GO ABOUT IT

Give an extra gift.

1. Think of someone special in your life whom you could give a gift to.
2. Ask a grown-up to help you buy or make a gift for this person.
3. Wrap the gift as a family and pray for the person who will be receiving it!

TALK ABOUT IT

- What's a gift you've given to someone else?
- How did you feel after giving that gift?
- Why does God want us to be generous?

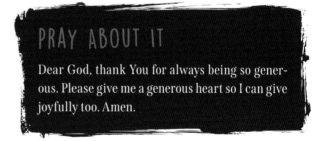

PRAY ABOUT IT

Dear God, thank You for always being so generous. Please give me a generous heart so I can give joyfully too. Amen.

LIGHT OF THE WORLD

Jesus spoke to the people once more and said, "I am the light of the world. If you follow me, you won't have to walk in darkness, because you will have the light that leads to life."
JOHN 8:12 NLT

What if people never grew up? Imagine a world with only babies and toddlers crawling around, drooling all over everything, and filling up their stinky diapers! Thankfully, humans *do* grow up, and because Jesus was fully God and fully human, He grew up too.

However, even though He was human, Jesus was a little different. We know that everyone in the world has sinned–everyone except Jesus.

When we disobey God and sin, our world can feel dark, lonely, and even scary. But Jesus brings light into dark places. He grew up and lived a perfect life. Then He died on the cross so that His perfect life would pay for our sins and we could be forgiven. But here's the miracle: Jesus didn't stay dead. He came back to life, and His light still shines today!

Want to know something really cool? We can share Jesus' light with the world! That's because Jesus' light lives inside every single person who follows Him. So if you're following Jesus, His light is shining in you right now.

READ ABOUT IT

Luke 24:1–6 NIrV

It was very early in the morning on the first day of the week. The women took the spices they had prepared. Then they went to the tomb. They found the stone rolled away from it. When they entered the tomb, they did not find the body of the Lord Jesus. They were wondering about this. Suddenly two men in clothes as bright as lightning stood beside them. The women were terrified. They bowed down with their faces to the ground. Then the men said to them, "Why do you look for the living among the dead? Jesus is not here! He has risen!"

You can read about Jesus' death in Luke 23:44–46.

GO ABOUT IT

Enjoy the many lights of Christmas.

1. Find out where you can see Christmas lights in your area.
2. When it starts getting dark outside, put on Christmas jammies and head out to view the lights as a family.
3. Talk about how Jesus came to be the Light of the World!

TALK ABOUT IT

- Why is sin a problem?
- Who is the Light of the World?
- How can we show Jesus' light to others?

PRAY ABOUT IT

Dear God, thank You for sending Jesus to light up the darkness in our world. Help me to shine His light to those around me. Amen.

DAY 25
OUR FOREVER SAVIOR

The Father has sent his Son to be the Savior of the world.
1 JOHN 4:14 NIrV

Presents under the tree, frosted Christmas cookies, and festive decorations are so much fun, aren't they? But those things aren't what Christmas is all about. Jesus is! He's the real reason we celebrate Christmas!

God loves the world so much that He sent us the greatest gift ever—a Savior who can keep us close to God, even after we sin. Jesus is this perfect Savior. He's our Rescuer, Leader, Teacher, and Friend. He's our Guide and the Prince of Peace. He is the Light of the World!

Jesus cares so much about you. He was born for you, and He wants to be close to you forever and ever. Maybe you've already decided to follow Jesus—that's awesome! But if you haven't yet, you can be sure that He's right there waiting for you to say *yes* to Him.

This Christmas, enjoy the small delights around you, but don't forget what Christmas is truly about. You can bring the hope, joy, peace, and love of Jesus with you into your celebrations. Shine His light everywhere you go, today and every day. Our forever Savior has been born.

Merry Christmas!

READ ABOUT IT

Luke 2:11–14 NIV

"Today in the town of David a Savior has been born to you; he is the Messiah, the Lord. This will be a sign to you: You will find a baby wrapped in cloths and lying in a manger."

Suddenly a great company of the heavenly host appeared with the angel, praising God and saying,

"Glory to God in the highest heaven, and on earth peace to those on whom his favor rests."

GO ABOUT IT

Celebrate the birth of our Savior with family and friends. Here are some ideas to keep Jesus at the center of your celebrations:

1. Read the story of Jesus' birth in Luke 2.
2. Pray and thank God for the gift of Jesus.
3. Bake a cake or cupcakes to celebrate Jesus' birthday.
4. Show Jesus' love through your words and actions.
5. Have lots of fun—remember, we can have joy because of Jesus!

PRAY ABOUT IT

Dear God, thank You for sending Jesus to be our Savior forever. Help me to share Jesus with others. Amen.

TALK ABOUT IT

- What is your favorite way to celebrate Christmas?
- Have you made the decision to follow Jesus and make Him your Savior?
- How can you show Jesus' hope, joy, peace, and love to others this Christmas?